Every Day

Written by Catherine DeVries
Illustrated by Kelly Pulley

CANDLE
BOOKS

The Beginner's Bible Every Day
Published in the UK in 2009 by Candle Books,
a publishing imprint of Lion Hudson plc

Worldwide co-edition organised and produced by Lion Hudson plc,
Wilkinson House, Jordan Hill Road, Oxford OX2 8DR England
Tel: +44 (0)1865 302750 Fax: +44 (0)1865 302757
Email: coed@lionhudson.com www.lionhudson.com

Distributed by Marston Book Services Ltd,
PO Box 269, Abingdon, Oxon OX14 4YN

USA edition published by Zonderkidz

Editor: Kristen Tuinstra
Art direction: Laura Maitner-Mason and Sarah Molegraaf
Cover and Interior Design: Laura Maitner-Mason

Presented to:

Abigail

From:

Joshua matthew Smart

OLD TESTAMENT

NEW TESTAMENT

God Made the world

There once was a boy who loved to go to his grandma's house. They liked finger painting. They painted pictures of people, animals, flowers and many other things. After their pictures were dry, they taped them to Grandma's refrigerator for everyone to see.

In the beginning, God created the heavens and the earth.

Genesis 1:1

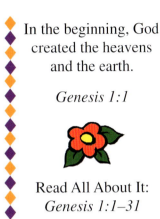

Read All About It:
Genesis 1:1–31

At the very beginning of time, God decided to make something. God made the sun, moon and stars. He made dry ground, plants and trees. He made all the animals – floppy-eared elephants, scurrying ants, tall giraffes and tiny kittens.

Finally, God made two people – a man named Adam and a woman named Eve. It took God 1-2-3-4-5-6 days to make the world and everything in it.

How wonderful it is to live in such a beautiful world! God's creation is here for all of us to see!

Idea

Name two or three things God made
when he created the world.

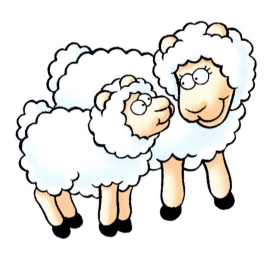

Verse to Remember

In the beginning, God created
the heavens and the earth.

Genesis 1:1

Hiding the Truth

There once was a boy who played ball in the house, even though his mum had told him not to. One day his ball bounced into a lamp and – *crash!* The lamp broke.

He tried to hide what he had done. But soon his mum found out the truth. She punished her little boy for disobeying and for breaking the lamp. But then she wiped his tears and told him that she still loved him… even though he had done a bad thing.

The woman… took some of the fruit and ate it. She also gave some to her husband, who was with her. And he ate it… They hid from the Lord… The Lord God said to Adam… "You ate the fruit of the tree that I commanded you about"… So the Lord God drove the man out of the Garden of Eden.

Genesis 3:6, 8, 17, 23

Read All About It: *Genesis 3:1–24*

In this Bible story, Adam and Eve did not obey God. He had told them not to eat fruit from one special tree. But they ate it anyway – *crunch!* Adam and Eve hid from God because they were afraid.

But God already knew the truth. He punished Adam and Eve for disobeying by eating from the tree. But he still loved them – even though they had done a bad thing.

Prayer

Dear God,
I'm sorry I don't always
listen or do the things I should.
Please help me follow you better,
and help me do what is good.
Amen.

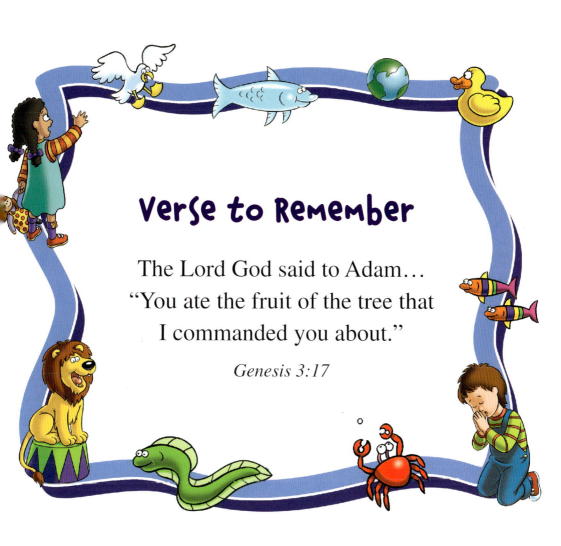

Verse to Remember

The Lord God said to Adam…
"You ate the fruit of the tree that
I commanded you about."

Genesis 3:17

Noah Had a Zoo

Have you ever been to the zoo? What animal do you like to watch the most? The monkeys – oo, oo, oo – love to chase each other and play! The elephants walk really slowly, swinging their trunks back and forth. And the lions open their mouths and yawn – what big teeth they have! In the zoo, we see many animals all in one place.

Noah did everything the Lord commanded him to do… He and his family… entered the ark to escape the waters of the flood… So did pairs of birds and pairs of all of the creatures that move along the ground… Rain fell on the earth for 40 days and 40 nights.

Genesis 7:5, 7–8, 12

Read All About It: *Genesis 6:5 – 8:22*

Noah's ark was like a zoo. God told Noah to bring two of every kind of animal onto the ark. Can you imagine how loud the animals were, making all their different animal sounds all day long? Imagine cockerels crowing, cows mooing, cats purring, dogs barking, bears growling, crickets chirping and frogs croaking… all at the same time!

Noah and his family took care of the animals inside the ark until they could safely go outside again. God loved Noah, his family and all the animals very much.

Good Man Noah

Tune: Old MacDonald

Good man Noah had an ark, E-I-E-I-O

And on that ark there were two _____
(cows, cats, dogs, bears, frogs), E-I-E-I-O

With a _____ , _____ here
(moo, meow, ruff, grrr, ribbit)

And a _____ , _____ there
(moo, meow, ruff, grrr, ribbit)

Here a _____ , there a _____ ,
(moo, meow, ruff, grrr, ribbit)

Everywhere a _____ , _____ ,
(moo, meow, ruff, grrr, ribbit)

Good man Noah had an ark, E-I-E-I-O.

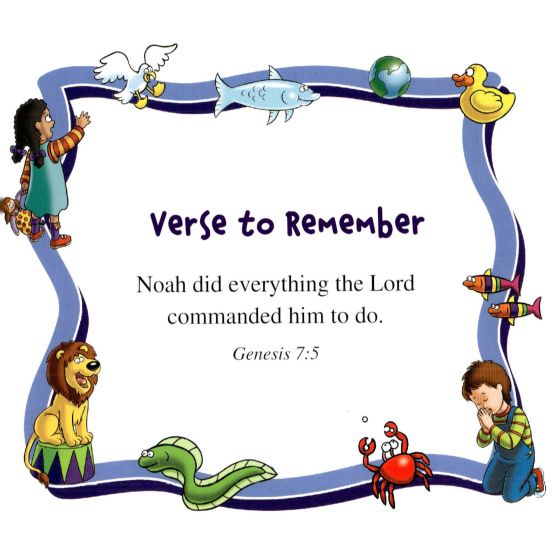

Verse to Remember

Noah did everything the Lord
commanded him to do.

Genesis 7:5

The Very First Rainbow

Look at this picture of a rainbow. See all the bright colours? There are bands of red and orange and yellow and blue. Have you ever seen a rainbow peek through the clouds after a rainstorm?

God said to Noah, "I have put my rainbow in the clouds. It will be the sign of the covenant between me and the earth. Sometimes when I bring clouds over the earth, a rainbow will appear in them. Then I will remember my covenant between me and you and every kind of living thing."

Genesis 9:13–15

Read All About It:
Genesis 9:8–15

Rainbows are soooo big and soooo pretty. They start in one place and arch way over to another place. Don't you wish you could touch one?

Did you know that the Bible tells us the story of the very first rainbow?

God put a rainbow in the sky as a sign to Noah. God promised he would never again send a flood that would cover the whole world.

When you see a rainbow, remember the promise God made to Noah long ago.

Idea

Draw and colour in a picture of a rainbow.
Which colours did you use?

Verse to Remember

"I have put my rainbow
in the clouds."

Genesis 9:13

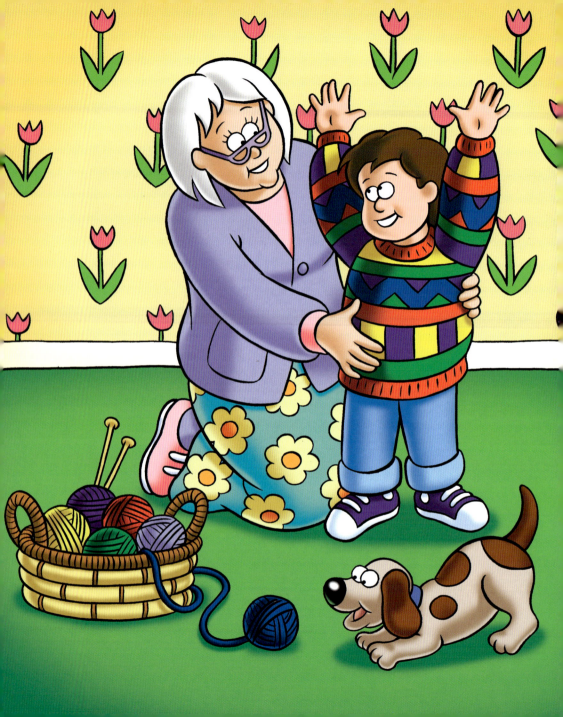

A Beautiful Robe

A boy's grandma wanted to make something very special for him. She wanted it to remind him of how much she loved him. She decided to knit him a jumper. When she gave the jumper to her grandson, she said, "Imagine that this warm jumper is me giving you a hug every time you wear it." The boy loved his jumper. It was his favourite thing to wear.

Jacob loved Joseph more than any of his other sons. Joseph had been born to him when he was old. Jacob made him a beautiful robe.

Genesis 37:3

Read All About It:
Genesis 37:1–11

Do you have a favourite jumper, jacket or shirt that you like to wear? Joseph did. It was his robe. Joseph loved his robe because his father made it just for him. Whenever he wore the robe, he could imagine that his father was giving him a hug. What colours do you see in Joseph's beautiful robe?

Idea

Put on your dressing gown or coat and pretend you are Joseph. Describe all of the different colours in your beautiful "robe".

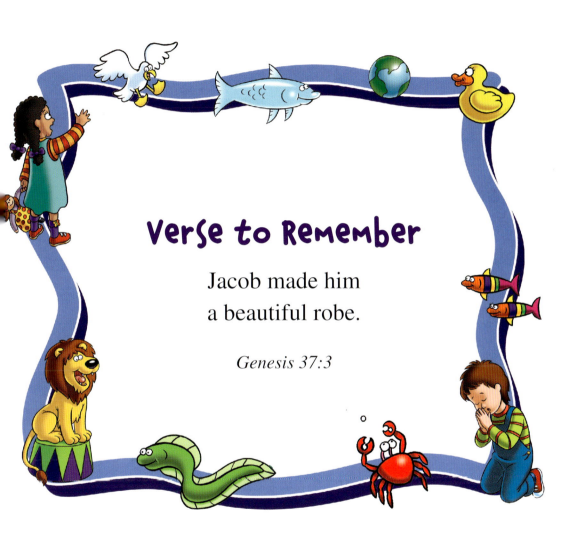

Verse to Remember

Jacob made him
a beautiful robe.

Genesis 37:3

Forgive Everybody

How do you feel when your friends or family members are mean to you? You feel sad, don't you? Sometimes people wait a long time before they say they're sorry. In fact, they might never say they're sorry. Still, you need to forgive people who hurt you. That takes a lot of love!

Joseph said to his brothers… "I am your brother Joseph. I'm the one you sold into Egypt. But don't be upset… God sent me… here to save your lives."

Genesis 45:4–5, 7

Forgive, just as the Lord forgave you.

Colossians 3:13

Read All About It:
Genesis 37:17–28, 45:1–11

Joseph's brothers were very mean to him.
They sold him as a slave.

But God helped Joseph. Joseph became a very
famous and powerful man in Egypt. He lived in
the palace with the pharaoh (the pharaoh was the
king).

When the people in the land had no food,
Joseph's brothers travelled to Egypt and asked
for his help. Joseph could have been mean to his
brothers after what they did to him. But Joseph
gave them the food they needed. And he decided
to forgive his brothers. That took a lot of love!

Idea

The next time someone is mean to you, remember Joseph's story. And remember to be kind to your friends and family members, too!

Verse to Remember

Forgive, just as the
Lord forgave you.

Colossians 3:13

Floating Safely

When you go swimming, you might wear armbands or a life jacket, right? These things help keep your head above the water. It's fun to float on your back. Oops, someone just splashed you! Sometimes you might sit on a rubber ring or an inflatable raft. You float this way and that way, drifting wherever the water takes you.

Moses' mother got a basket that was made out of the stems of tall grass. She coated it with tar. Then she placed the child in it. She put the basket in the tall grass that grew along the bank of the Nile River… Pharaoh's daughter… saw the basket in the tall grass… he became her son.

Exodus 2:3, 5, 10

Read All About It:
Exodus 2:1–10

Baby Moses needed to be kept away from wicked Pharaoh. Moses' mother helped him get away safely. She set him in a basket on a river. Baby Moses floated this way and that way, drifting wherever the water took him. His big sister, Miriam, watched from the river's edge.

A princess saw the basket as it floated by. When she looked inside and saw baby Moses, she decided he should live in the royal palace with her. And, as his mother had hoped, God watched over Moses and kept him safe.

He's Got the whole world in His Hands

Traditional

He's got the whole world in his hands. (*4 times*)
He's got the little bitty baby in his hands, (*3 times*)
he's got the whole world in his hands.
He's got you and me, sister, in his hands, (*3 times*)
he's got the whole world in his hands.
He's got you and me, brother, in his hands, (*3 times*)
he's got the whole world in his hands.

Verse to Remember

She put the basket in the tall grass
that grew along the bank
of the Nile River.

Exodus 2:3

47

Campfires and Burning Bushes

Have you ever sat beside a campfire? The logs on the fire crackle and pop. To keep the fire going, you need to keep adding logs to it. The flames from the fire flicker. But watch out! It's really hot!

It's fun to sit around a campfire and think about God – maybe even sing songs to him.

The angel of the Lord appeared to him from inside a burning bush. Moses saw that the bush was on fire. But it didn't burn up… The Lord said, "I have seen my people suffer in Egypt… So now, go. I am sending you to Pharaoh. I want you to bring the Israelites out of Egypt."

Exodus 3:2, 7, 10

Read All About It:
Exodus 3:1–21

In this Bible story, Moses watched a fire too. It was a burning bush. It must have crackled and popped as the flames burned the wood. But you know what? The bush never burned up.

As Moses watched the burning bush, another amazing thing happened. Moses heard a voice. It was God! God talked to Moses from out of the burning bush. He told Moses to help God's people get away from a place called Egypt. So Moses went to Egypt to help.

Idea

Ask your mum or dad (or another adult) to light a candle for you. As you watch the candle flame, think about how Moses felt when God talked to him from the fire.

Verse to Remember

The angel of the Lord appeared to him from inside a burning bush. Moses saw that the bush was on fire. But it didn't burn up.

Exodus 3:2

walking Through the Sea

When we go to the zoo, we see fish and other water animals in big tanks called *aquariums*. We watch the fish swish their tails back and forth as they swim. We see crabs scurry along the bottom. We feel like we are swimming because of the water all around us. But we don't even get wet.

Then Moses reached his hand out over the Red Sea. All that night the Lord pushed the sea back with a strong east wind. He turned the sea into dry land… The people of Israel went through the sea on dry ground. There was a wall of water on their right side and on their left.

Exodus 14:21–22

Read All About It:
Exodus 13:18 – 14:31

As Moses led the Israelites away from Egypt, wicked Pharaoh chased them. The people stood on the edge of the Red Sea. What were the Israelites going to do?

God helped Moses and the Israelites that day. God split the huge sea into two parts – almost like two big aquariums. As the people walked through, they may have seen fish swishing their tails as they swam. They may have seen crabs scurrying along the bottom. Moses and the Israelites must have felt like they were swimming, but they never even got wet. God helped them get away from wicked Pharaoh. Hurray!

Idea

Look at an aquarium or fish bowl.
Put your face right up to it.
Now you know how God's people felt!

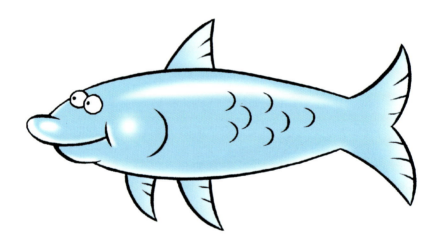

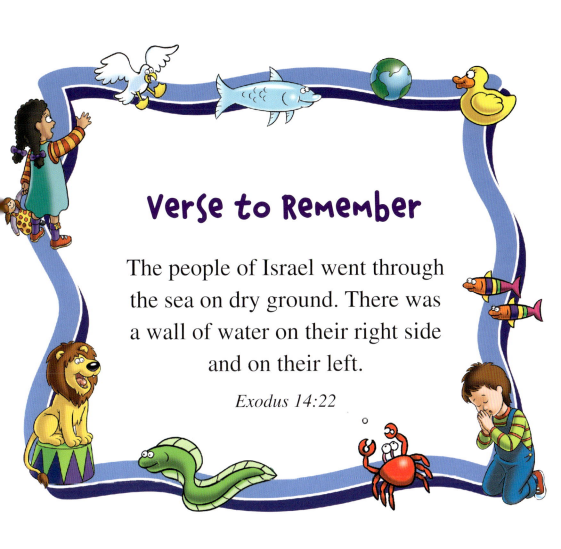

Verse to Remember

The people of Israel went through the sea on dry ground. There was a wall of water on their right side and on their left.

Exodus 14:22

Follow the Rules

Wipe your feet. Don't run in the house. Brush your teeth.

Rules, rules, rules! Sometimes you get tired of them, don't you? But rules are there for a reason. What would happen if you didn't ever wipe your feet? What could get broken if you ran through the house? And what do you think would happen if you never brushed your teeth? Rules help you live the way you should.

"'Love the Lord your God with all your heart and with all your soul… and with all your mind… Love your neighbour as you love yourself.'"

Matthew 22:37, 39

Read All About It:
Exodus 20:1–17

God has rules in the Bible, too. Some of them are called the Ten Commandments. These rules help us know how God wants us to live. But do you know what is the most important rule of all? To love God with all of your heart, soul and mind. The next most important rule is to love others as much as you love yourself. That takes a lot of love, doesn't it?

Song

The B-I-B-L-E

Traditional

The B-I-B-L-E, yes,
that's the book for me.
I stand alone on the Word of God,
the B-I-B-L-E!

Verse to Remember

Love the Lord your God with all your heart and with all your soul… and with all your mind.

Matthew 22:37

when You're Hungry

"I'm hungry!" Have you ever said that? Yes, we all have! When you are hungry, your tummy needs food. It might even make rumble grumble noises that mean, "Feed me!" Thank goodness you never have to wait too long before you get something to eat. And you usually have a choice of what you'd like to eat. Sandwiches, fruit, pizza, ice cream – what's your favourite thing to eat?

The people of Israel said to Moses and Aaron, "You have brought us out into this desert. You must want this entire community to die of hunger." Then the Lord spoke to Moses. He said, "I will rain down bread from heaven for you."… The people of Israel called the bread manna.

Exodus 16:3–4, 31

Read All About It:
Exodus 16:1–31

Well, God's people in this Bible story were feeling very hungry. They were on a trip, and they didn't know how long they would be away. Their tummies were making rumble grumble noises that meant, "Feed me!" So they said to God, "We're hungry!" God sent food called *manna* that fell down from the sky like snowflakes. Manna tasted like bread sweetened with honey.

Even in the desert, God took care of his people and fed them every single day. Praise God for food!

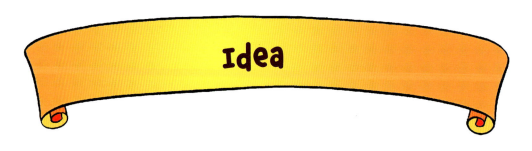

Idea

Pretend that you are picking up manna.
Break some bread into small pieces.
Then sprinkle the pieces on the table.
Get a paper bag and pick up all the pieces
of bread. Now eat them as part of your lunch.

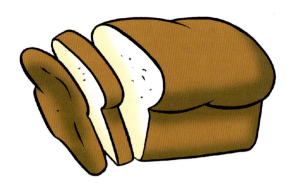

Verse to Remember

"I will rain down bread from heaven for you."

Exodus 16:4

Everybody Has a Job to Do

What job do you want to have when you grow up? Do you want to be a firefighter, a teacher, or how about an artist? It's fun to think of all the different jobs you could have when you grow up.

But guess what? You have a job to do right now! Your job is to love God. God wants you to show your love for others by being nice to them, obeying your parents, and sharing with your friends. Those things are all part of your job.

Eli realized that the Lord was calling the boy. So Eli told Samuel… "If someone calls out to you again, say, 'Speak, Lord. I'm listening.'"… The Lord came and… called out, just as he had done the other times… Then Samuel replied, "Speak. I'm listening."

1 Samuel 3:8–10

Read All About It: *1 Samuel 3:1–10*

73

In this Bible story, God talked to a boy named Samuel. God had a job for Samuel to do. Samuel listened, and worked as God's prophet for the rest of his life.

You don't have to be grown up before you can start working for God. When you do good things for other people, you are doing what God wants you to do.

Idea

Think of one nice thing you can do today
for your mum, dad, brother or sister, or a friend.
Now, go and do it!

Verse to Remember

Samuel replied,
"Speak. I'm listening."

1 Samuel 3:10

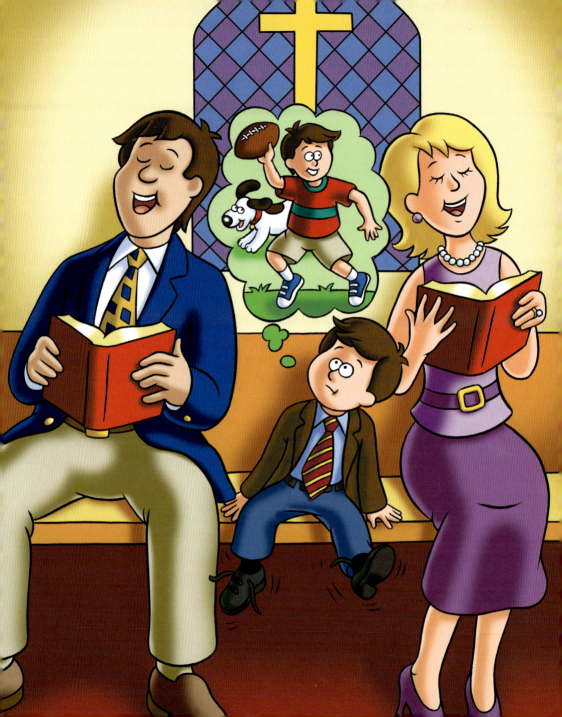

God Can Help

Do you ever feel like some things are just too hard to do? How about sitting still during church? That's really hard! Or what about trying to be shhhh quiet when someone else is sleeping? You'd probably rather run around and laugh and giggle and talk, talk, talk!

Being quiet just isn't much fun. But sometimes you have to do things even when they are hard to do.

David said to Goliath, "You are coming to fight against me with a sword, a spear and a javelin. But I'm coming against you in the name of the Lord who rules over all… This very day the Lord will hand you over to me."

1 Samuel 17:45–46

Read All About It:
1 Samuel 17:1–58

This Bible story is about a boy named David.
He needed to do something that was really hard.
He had to fight a giant who stood about as high
as your bedroom ceiling. Wow, that is really tall!

Was David scared? No! David trusted God. He didn't let the big giant make him feel afraid. He knew that God would help him. And God did. He helped David knock down the giant with a stone. David won!

Prayer

Dear God,
Please help me remember
that you're always there.
Help me know
that you'll always care.
When I have to do
things I think are hard,
help me to keep trying –
keep me going, Lord.
Amen.

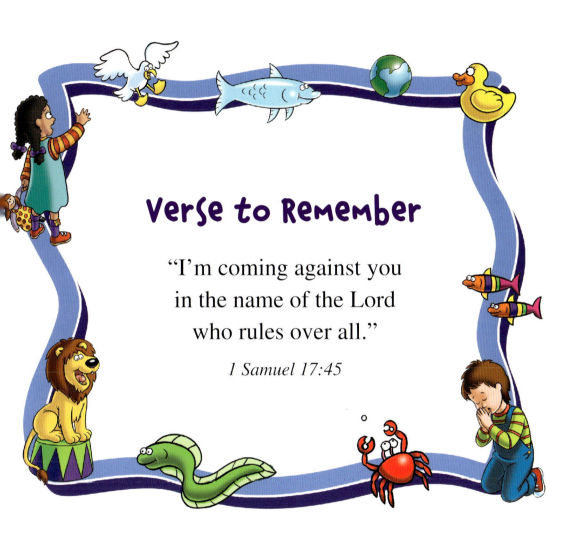

Verse to Remember

"I'm coming against you
in the name of the Lord
who rules over all."

1 Samuel 17:45

Daniel and the Lions' Den

It's exciting to see lions at the zoo or at the circus. They are so big and so fierce! Their tails swish back and forth as they walk on their big paws. But we wouldn't want to go inside a lion's house, and we wouldn't want a real lion to go inside our house.

The heavens tell about the glory of God. The skies show that his hands created them. Day after day they speak about it. Night after night they make it known. But they don't speak or use words.

Psalm 19:1–3

Read All About It:
Psalm 19:1–14

Some leaders said to King Darius, "Don't let any of your people pray to any god or man except to you. If they do, throw them into the lions' den." Daniel… went to his room three times a day to pray… Daniel was brought out and thrown into the lions' den… The next day Daniel told the king, "My God sent his angel. And his angel shut the mouths of the lions."

Daniel 6:7, 10, 16, 22

Read All About It:
Daniel 6:1–28

In this Bible story, Daniel was thrown into the lions' den. No cages or bars kept Daniel safe from the lions. They swished their tails back and forth as they walked on their big paws around Daniel. But Daniel was not scared. God sent an angel to

keep the lions' mouths shut so they wouldn't hurt
Daniel. God knew that Daniel needed his help.
And God saved Daniel from danger.

God can help us too when we feel scared. All
we need to do is pray to God and ask for his help.

Idea

Roar like a lion! Now have someone
pretend he or she is an angel. As soon as the
angel touches your mouth, stop roaring.

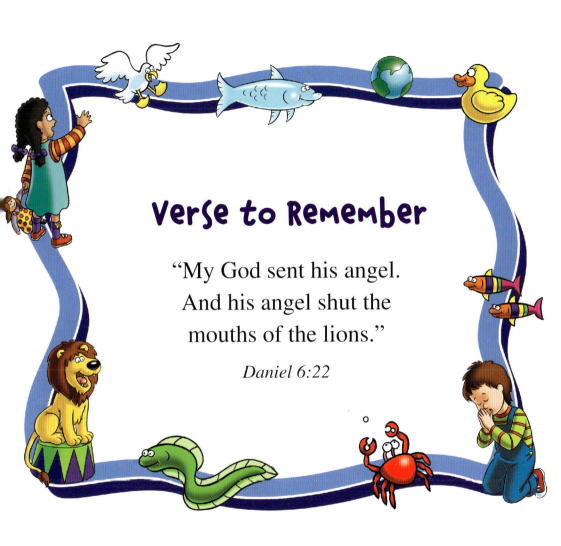

Verse to Remember

"My God sent his angel.
And his angel shut the
mouths of the lions."

Daniel 6:22

Time-out

When we do something that's bad, we sometimes need to have quiet time. Maybe we have to sit in a chair, or go to our room. Time-outs give us a chance to think about what we did wrong and remember what's right. We wait and wait… and finally the time's up! Then we try to do what's right.

The Lord sent a huge fish to swallow Jonah. And Jonah was inside the fish for three days and three nights. From inside the fish Jonah prayed to the Lord his God… The Lord gave the fish a command. And it spat Jonah up onto dry land.

Jonah 1:17 – 2:1, 10

Read All About It:
Jonah 1:17 – 2:10

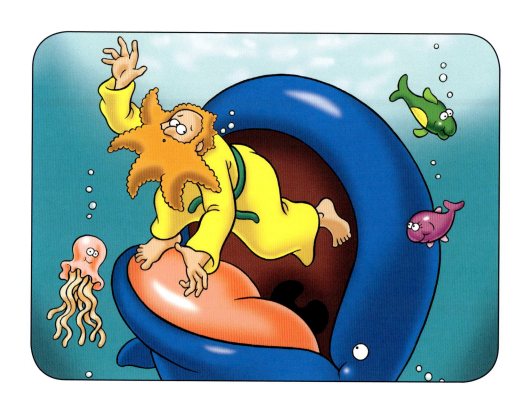

In this Bible story, God made a man named Jonah have some quiet time. But Jonah didn't have to sit in a chair or go to his room. After he disobeyed God, Jonah spent his time-out in the belly of a fish! That's right. A big fish swallowed Jonah whole. *Gulp!*

Inside the fish's stomach, Jonah prayed to God. He told God that only God could save him.

Then he sang a song of thanks. Finally,
after three days went by, God made the fish spit
Jonah out onto dry land. Then Jonah obeyed God.
Wouldn't you?

Idea

Lie on the floor and cover yourself with a blanket. Then imagine that you are Jonah in the belly of the fish. Is it dark? Is it quiet? Is it lonely? After a few minutes, get up and go wherever you want to go in the house. Which did you like doing better and why?

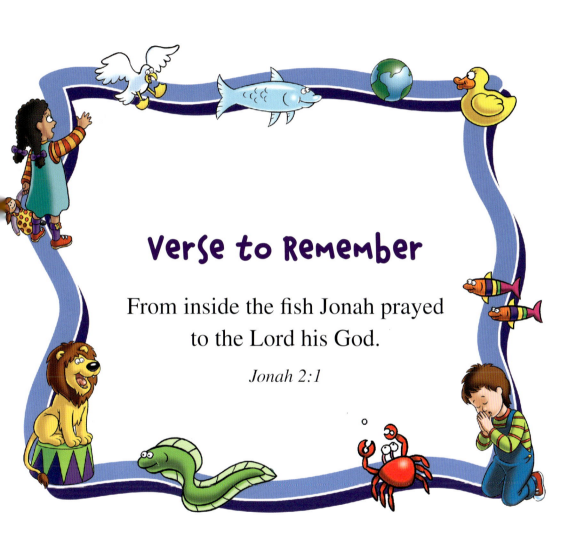

Verse to Remember

From inside the fish Jonah prayed
to the Lord his God.

Jonah 2:1

Baby Jesus is Born

There once was a girl who, at Christmas time, loved to sleep on the sofa and watch the twinkling lights on the Christmas tree. Her mum would often wrap a quilt around her on those special nights. They would sit next to each other and talk for a long time. Sometimes the girl would ask her mum to tell her a story.

While Joseph and Mary were in Bethlehem, the time came for the child to be born. She gave birth to her first baby. It was a boy. She wrapped him in large strips of cloth. Then she placed him in a manger. There was no room for them in the inn.

Luke 2:6–7

Read All About It:
Luke 2:1–7

One of the best stories in the Bible is when baby Jesus was born. He had no bed – only a manger, which held food for the animals. He had no house – only a stable. He saw no Christmas tree – only the twinkling stars that shone in

through the door and windows. His mother Mary loved him very, very much. Mary tucked baby Jesus in for the night and said, "Goodnight, baby Jesus. Goodnight."

Away in a Manger

Anonymous

Away in a manger, no crib for a bed,
the little Lord Jesus lay down his sweet head.
The stars in the sky looked down where he lay,
the little Lord Jesus asleep on the hay.

Verse to Remember

Then she placed him
in a manger. There was no
room for them in the inn.

Luke 2:7

The Lord's Prayer

When we close our eyes and fold our hands, what are we getting ready to do? Yes, we are going to pray. Often we pray at the table before a meal or right before we go to bed.

We say all sorts of different things to God when we pray.

Jesus said, "This is how you should pray. 'Our Father in heaven, may your name be honoured. May your kingdom come. May what you want to happen be done on earth as it is done in heaven. Give us today our daily bread… '"

Matthew 6:9–11

Read All About It:
Matthew 6:5–15

When Jesus lived in the world long ago, he prayed to God often. He said that praying is very important for us to do. He taught us a prayer that is called the Lord's Prayer.

Our Father in heaven,
hallowed be your name,
your kingdom come,
your will be done,
on earth as in heaven.
Give us today our daily bread.
Forgive us our sins
as we forgive those who sin against us.
Lead us not into temptation
but deliver us from evil.
For the kingdom, the power,
and the glory are yours
now and for ever.
Amen.

Idea

Practise saying the Lord's Prayer with
a parent or friend. Pick a certain time of day
when you say it – perhaps right before you go to
bed at night or on your way to school.

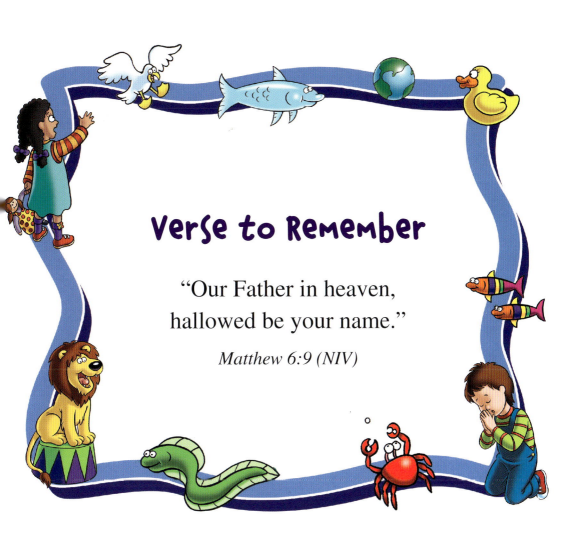

Verse to Remember

"Our Father in heaven,
hallowed be your name."

Matthew 6:9 (NIV)

Don't worry

What are we going to do today?
Where did my favourite toy go?
When will you read me a story?
Why do I have to go to bed
now?

Have you ever asked any of
these questions? You want to
know everything that's going to
happen. But you don't need to
worry. Jesus doesn't want you
to worry.

"Don't worry about your life and what you will eat or drink… Look at the birds of the air. They don't plant or gather crops… But your Father who is in heaven feeds them… Put God's kingdom first. Do what he wants you to do. Then all of those things will also be given to you."

Matthew 6:25–26, 33

Read All About It:
Matthew 6:25–34

Jesus said to look at the birds. They sing and tweet and fly up in the air. They don't have refrigerators or kitchens to store food in. But they never worry about when they'll eat dinner – not even a little bit. Do you know why? Because God takes care of them.

Yes, God loves the birds. And he loves you, too! If God can take care of the birds outside, how much more will he take care of you? Lots and lots! So don't worry. Instead, think of what the birds do!

Idea

Pretend that you are a bird.
Flap your wings and sing, "Tweet, tweet."
You could even eat some cereal
and pretend it is birdseed!

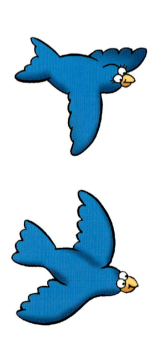

Verse to Remember

"But put God's kingdom first.
Do what he wants you to do."

Matthew 6:33

when you're Afraid

Thunderstorms can be scary! The rain comes down from the sky. It sounds like little hammers hitting the roof – *bang, bang, bang, bang, bang!* The sun hides behind the gloomy sky. The wind whooshes outside, and when you look out of the window you see trees bending back and forth, back and forth.

The disciples… said, "Lord! Save us! We're going to drown!" Jesus replied, "Your faith is so small! Why are you so afraid?" Then Jesus got up and ordered the winds and the waves to stop. It became completely calm. The disciples were amazed.

Matthew 8:25–27

When I'm afraid, I will trust in you.

Psalm 56:3

Read All About It: *Matthew 8:23–27*

Some friends of Jesus didn't like thunderstorms either. They were in a boat when, suddenly, rain came down from the sky. The boat swayed back and forth, back and forth, as the wind whipped up the waves. "Jesus, help us! Our boat is going to sink!" they cried.

Jesus stood up and told the storm to be quiet. Right away the rain stopped falling from the sky. The sun came back out. The whooshing wind was still. The boat stopped swaying back and forth.

Isn't Jesus amazing?

Idea

To remember this story, draw a picture of Jesus standing in the boat with calm water all around. Be sure to draw the disciples' smiling faces! The next time you're afraid, remember this drawing. Jesus can help you.

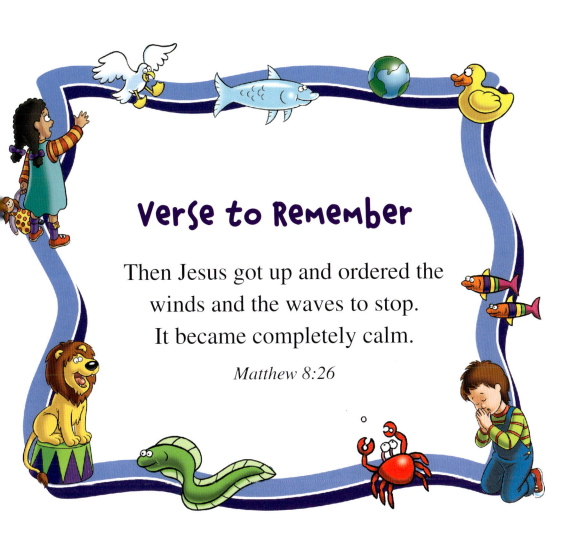

Verse to Remember

Then Jesus got up and ordered the
winds and the waves to stop.
It became completely calm.

Matthew 8:26

Nothing is Too Hard for Jesus

Have you ever been to a hospital? People go to the hospital for different reasons. Some go there to have babies. Other people go there because they have been hurt. Still others go there because they are ill. The doctors and nurses try to help these people get well. Many people get better, but some people don't.

Someone came from the house of Jairus… "Your daughter is dead," the messenger said… Jesus said to Jairus, "Don't be afraid. Just believe. She will be healed." When he arrived at the house of Jairus… Jesus took her by the hand and said, "My child, get up!" Her spirit returned, and right away she stood up.

Luke 8:49–51, 54–55

Read All About It:
Luke 8:40–56

In this Bible story, a man named Jairus had a daughter who was very ill. Jairus believed that Jesus could help his daughter get better. But the little girl died before Jesus could see her. Oh, how sad this father was! But it wasn't too late. Jesus went to Jairus' house, and he brought the little girl back to life. It was a miracle!

When Jesus lived on earth, he helped a lot of sick people get better. He even brought people back to life, like this little girl. Jesus, God's Son, is the best healer of all time.

Idea

Do you know someone who is ill?
Make that person a card and
draw a picture on the front of it.
Pray to Jesus and ask him
to help this person get better.

Verse to Remember

Jesus said to Jairus,
"Don't be afraid. Just believe.
She will be healed."

Luke 8:50

Jesus Did a Miracle!

One day, when a little girl went to school, she forgot to take her lunch box. She wondered, *How will I make it through the day without eating anything?*

When lunchtime came, some of her classmates helped her. One boy gave her half of his sandwich. One girl gave her a bright red apple. Her teacher gave her some milk. They all shared. And they all had enough to eat that day!

Jesus… said to Philip, "Where can we buy bread for these people to eat?"… Andrew… said, "Here is a boy with five small loaves of barley bread. He also has two small fish. But how far will that go in such a large crowd?"… Then Jesus took the loaves and gave thanks. He gave the people as much as they wanted.

John 6:5, 8–9, 11

Read All About It:
John 6:1–15

127

In this Bible story, a boy shared his lunch
with Jesus. The people who had been listening to
Jesus were getting hungry. This boy had a lunch,
but in it were only five bread loaves and two fish.
He gave all of his food to Jesus.

Then Jesus made a miracle happen. From that little boy's lunch, he made enough lunch for everyone. All the people had plenty to eat that day – more than 5,000 of them!

The next time you eat something,
share half of it with someone else.
Then tell them the story of the little boy
who shared, and the miracle Jesus
did with that food.

Verse to Remember

Then Jesus took the
loaves and gave thanks.

John 6:11

Lost!

There once was a girl who went to the store with her mum. They had fun shopping for all kinds of things. One time, in the middle of seeing this and seeing that, the girl looked up and discovered – Oh no! – she was lost! But soon her mum came round the corner. The worried looks on their faces turned into smiles when they saw each other again.

Jesus said, "Suppose one of you has 100 sheep and loses one of them. Won't he leave the 99 in the open country? Won't he go and look for the one lost sheep until he finds it? When he finds it, he… will say, 'Be joyful with me. I have found my lost sheep.'"

Luke 15:4–6

Read All About It:
Luke 15:4–7

This Bible story is about sheep. Younger
sheep love to run and prance in green fields.
What fun it is to play! Sometimes sheep look up
and discover – Oh no! – they are lost! But soon
their shepherd goes out and finds them.

God knows where everybody is all the time. If we ask him, he can help us find each other when wc get lost. All we need to do is trust that he will help.

Prayer

The Lord is my shepherd,
and I am his sheep.
He watches over me
even when I sleep.

Watch over me, Lord
as I prance and play.
Watch over me, Lord,
by night and by day.
Amen.

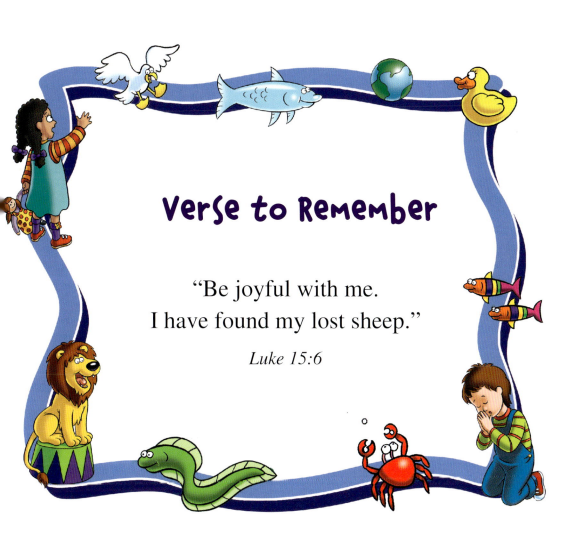

Verse to Remember

"Be joyful with me.
I have found my lost sheep."

Luke 15:6

Being Sorry

One day, a little boy took his crayons and scribbled up and down the family-room wall. When he tried to clean the wall, the crayon just smeared. "What will I do now?" he cried. Tears filled his eyes.

The little boy went to his dad and told him he was sorry. His dad was not happy about the crayon marks. But he was glad that his little boy felt sorry. His dad loved him so much!

The father divided his property between his two sons… The younger son… wasted his money on wild living. He spent everything he had… He said… "I will get up and go back to my father. I will say to him, 'Father… I have sinned against you.'"… His father… ran to him. He threw his arms around him and kissed him.

Luke 15:12–14, 17–18, 20

Read All About It: *Luke 15:11–32*

This Bible story is about a young man who did some wrong things. He left his home and went far away and wasted all his money. Then he went back to his house to tell his dad that he was sorry

for what he had done. But before he got there, his dad ran out to meet him. Oh, was the father glad his son had come back to apologize. He loved his son so much!

Prayer

I'm sorry, Jesus, that I sinned.
Please forgive me, I pray.
Help me know what to do
today, tomorrow and always.
Amen.

Verse to Remember

His father… ran to him.
He threw his arms around
him and kissed him.

Luke 15:20

Thank You!

When we feel ill, it's really hard to be happy because we can't do all the things we love to do. Sometimes we are unwell for a long time. But when we start to feel better, we want to jump up and down because we're so happy!

As Jesus was going into a village, ten men met him. They had a skin disease… Jesus saw them and said, "Go. Show yourselves to the priests"… When one of them saw that he was healed, he came back. He praised God in a loud voice… Jesus asked, "Weren't all ten healed? Where are the other nine?"

Luke 17:12–17

Read All About It:
Luke 17:11–19

145

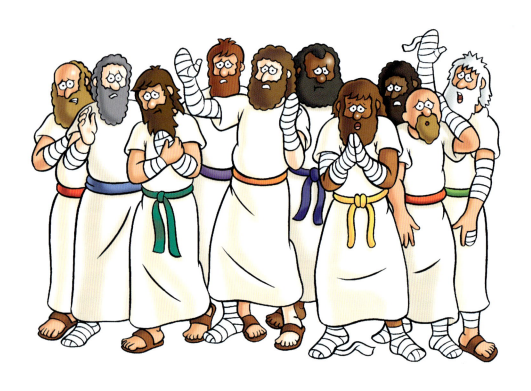

In Bible times, some people used to get ill
with sores all over their bodies. One day Jesus
saw ten men who had this skin disease. Jesus felt
sorry for them. Can you guess what he did? He
healed them. All of their sores disappeared! They
could now go back to their homes, their families

and their work. They probably jumped up and down because they were so happy! But, as happy as they were, only one man came back to thank Jesus.

Remember to pray to God and thank him for watching over us.

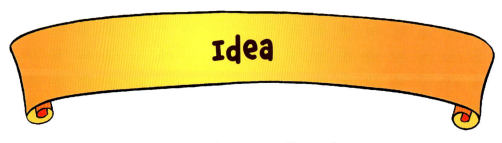

Idea

Jump up and down five times.
Each time you jump, say,
"Thank you, Jesus!"

Verse to Remember

When one of them saw that
he was healed, he came back.
He praised God in a loud voice.

Luke 17:15

Jesus Loves You

There once was a boy and girl who loved to welcome their dad home from work. They would rush to the door and say, "Daddy, Daddy" this and "Daddy, Daddy" that. Their daddy would scoop them up in his arms and then sit with them snuggled in his lap. How wonderful they felt in their daddy's arms. He would look at his happy children, and his eyes would twinkle with tender love for them.

Some people brought little children to Jesus. They wanted him to place his hands on the children and pray for them. But the disciples told the people to stop. Jesus said, "Let the little children come to me. Don't keep them away. The kingdom of heaven belongs to people like them."

Matthew 19:13–14

Read All About It:
Matthew 19:13–15

In this Bible story, the children felt the same way about Jesus. They were so glad to see him. They probably rushed to his side and said, "Jesus, Jesus" this and "Jesus, Jesus" that. He probably scooped them up and then sat with them snuggled in his lap. How wonderful they must have felt in Jesus' arms. As he looked at all the happy children, his eyes must have twinkled with tender love for them.

Jesus loves you, too!

Jesus Loves Me

Anna Bartlett Warner, 1860

Jesus loves me, this I know,
for the Bible tells me so.
Little ones to him belong,
they are weak, but he is strong.
Yes, Jesus loves me, (*3 times*)
the Bible tells me so.

Verse to Remember

Jesus said, "Let the
little children come to me.
Don't keep them away."

Matthew 19:14

Oh, to Be Taller!

Have you ever wished you were taller? Then you wouldn't have to drink out of the lower drinking fountain. You wouldn't have to stand on a step to be high enough. But don't worry, you're still growing.

Zacchaeus wanted to see who Jesus was. But he was a short man… So he ran ahead and climbed a sycamore-fig tree… Jesus reached the spot where Zacchaeus was. He looked up and said, "Zacchaeus, come down at once. I must stay at your house today."

Luke 19:3–5

Read All About It:
Luke 19:1–10

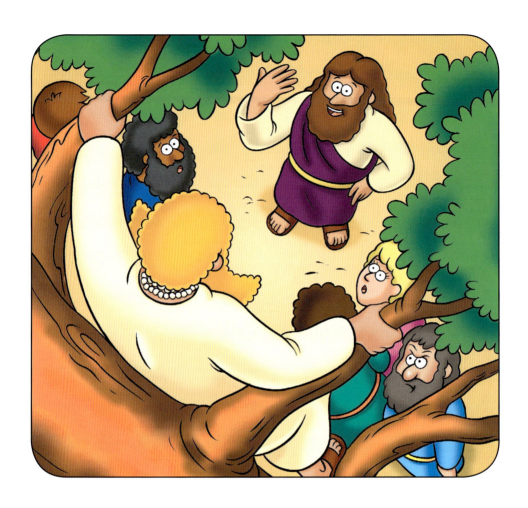

Zacchaeus was a very short man. He wanted
to see Jesus. But too many taller people stood in
the way. So you know what he did? He climbed
a tree! Jesus saw him up in the tree and said to
Zacchaeus, "I must stay at your house today."

Jesus doesn't look at how short or how tall we are. He loves short people and tall people. He loves older people and young children. And he wants us to be kind to each other.

Zacchaeus

Traditional

Zacchaeus was a wee little man,
and a wee little man was he.
He climbed up in a sycamore tree,
for the Lord he wanted to see.
And as the Saviour passed that way,
he looked up in the tree.
And he said, "Zacchaeus, you come down.
For I'm going to your house today,
for I'm going to your house today."

Verse to Remember

"Zaccheaus, come down at once. I must stay at your house today."

Luke 19:5

Jesus Died to Pay for Our Sins

Bath time is fun time! As the water streams out from the tap and tumbles into the tub, you climb in. *Splish splash… kersploosh!* You scrub-scrub-scrub and guess what? Your body is clean again! All the dirt on your body has washed off.

Christ died for sins once and for all time. The One who did what is right died for those who don't do right. He died to bring you to God. His body was put to death. But the Holy Spirit brought him back to life.

1 Peter 3:18

Read All About It:
1 Peter 3:16–18, 21–22

163

It feels great to be clean on the outside, but it feels even better to be clean on the inside. In other words, it feels great when we know our sins are forgiven. But how can we be forgiven for all the bad things we do and say?

Through Jesus! Jesus is God's very own Son. He lived on this earth, and he did a wonderful, incredible thing. Jesus died for us on a cross. He paid for all our sins. He went through a lot of pain, and he even gave up his life for us. But there's a happy ending. You'll learn all about it in the next Bible story.

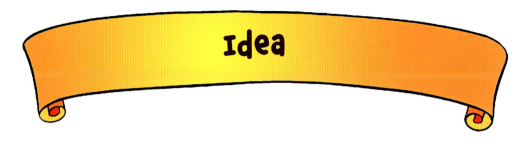

Idea

The next time you've finished having a bath, look at the dirty water and imagine that it is your sins. Then take the plug out and watch the water run out of the bathtub. Think about Jesus as being like the plughole, taking your sins away.

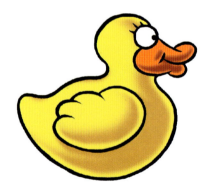

Verse to Remember

Christ died for sins
once and for all time.

1 Peter 3:18

Jesus is Alive!

When people want flowers to come up in the spring, they plant seeds in the ground. The seeds don't look alive. They are brown and hard. They don't look like flowers at all. But then in the spring, up come the flowers. How beautiful and alive they are!

An angel of the Lord came down from heaven… He rolled back the stone and sat on it. His body shone like lightning… The angel said to the women, "Don't be afraid. I know that you are looking for Jesus, who was crucified. He is not here! He has risen, just as he said he would!"

Matthew 28:2–6

Read All About It:
Matthew 28:1–20

Now think about Jesus. After Jesus died, he was buried. People put him in a tomb and rolled a huge stone in front of it. They thought Jesus was gone for ever. But three days later, an angel rolled the stone away. Jesus came out from the tomb. Jesus was alive again!

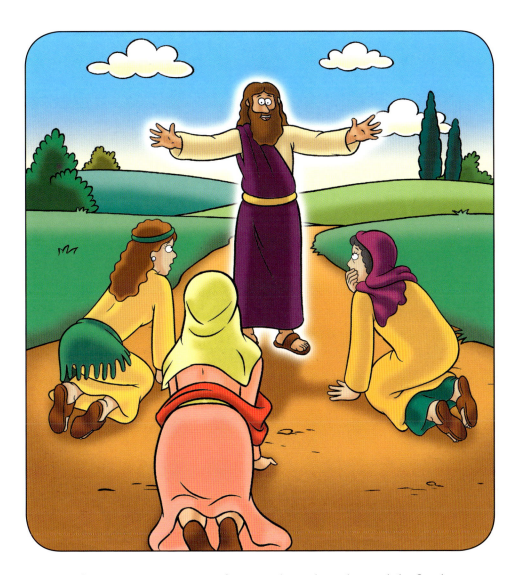

When Jesus rose from the dead and left the tomb, he set us free from our sins. That's the most wonderful news in the whole Bible!

Song

Christ the Lord is Risen Today

Charles Wesley, 1739

Christ the Lord is risen today, *Alleluia!*
Sons of men and angels say, *Alleluia!*
Raise your joys and triumphs high, *Alleluia!*
Sing, you heavens, and earth reply, *Alleluia!*

Verse to Remember

"He is not here! He has risen,
just as he said he would!"

Matthew 28:6

Jesus Goes to Heaven

Have you ever played the game Pass it On? One person tells someone a message. Then that person tells another person, until the message has gone all the way round a circle of people. The last person who gets the message says what the message is. It's a fun game!

Jesus appeared to the disciples… He said to them, "Go into all the world. Preach the good news to everyone. Anyone who believes and is baptized will be saved. But anyone who does not believe will be punished."… When the Lord Jesus finished speaking to them, he was taken up into heaven.

Mark 16:14–16, 19

Read All About It:
Mark 16:9–20

After Jesus rose from the dead, he told some women to pass on the message that he was alive. And they did! Later, Jesus appeared to the disciples. Jesus knew he wouldn't be on the earth much longer. He was soon going back to heaven. So Jesus gave his friends a message and asked them to pass it on. Jesus' followers told others about Jesus so they could learn about Jesus and become Christians, too.

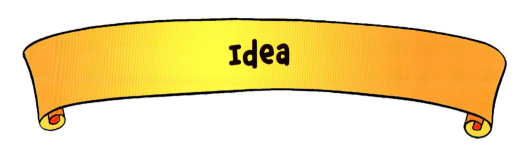

Idea

Play Pass it On with your family.
Say, "Jesus loves you! Pass it on!"

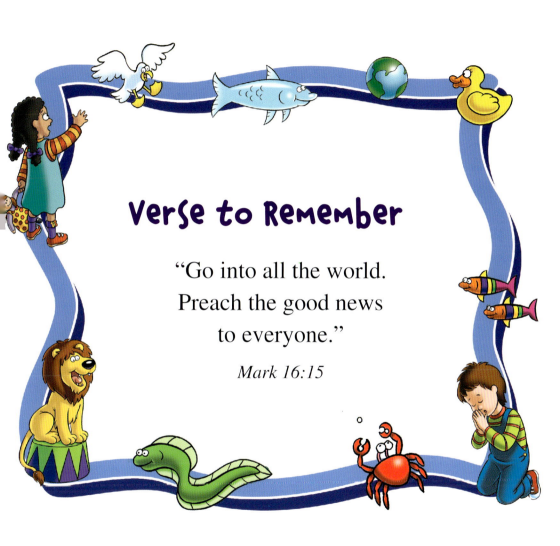

Verse to Remember

"Go into all the world.
Preach the good news
to everyone."

Mark 16:15

Jesus will Come Back

Do you remember the last time your grandparents visited you? They packed up their things and kissed you goodbye. Maybe you stood outside and waved as they drove away.

If your grandparents live close by, you probably weren't very sad. You knew you'd see them again soon. But if they live very far away, you may have been very sad to see them go.

Jesus… was taken up to heaven… Suddenly two men dressed in white clothing stood beside them. "Men of Galilee," they said, "why do you stand there looking at the sky? Jesus has been taken away from you into heaven. But he will come back in the same way you saw him go."

Acts 1:9–11

Read All About It:
Acts 1:3–11

The people in this Bible story had to say goodbye to Jesus. A big cloud came down and took Jesus up into the sky.

Two angels told the people who were watching not to worry. They promised that Jesus would come back to earth some day. And when he came back, he would come in the same way he left.

When he comes again, Jesus will take all of his people – all Christians from around the world – to heaven to be with him. What a wonderful day that will be!

Praise Him, All ye Little Children

Traditional

Praise him, praise him, all ye little children,
God is love, God is love. (*repeat*)
Love him, love him, all ye little children,
God is love, God is love. (*repeat*)
Thank him, thank him, all ye little children,
God is love, God is love. (*repeat*)

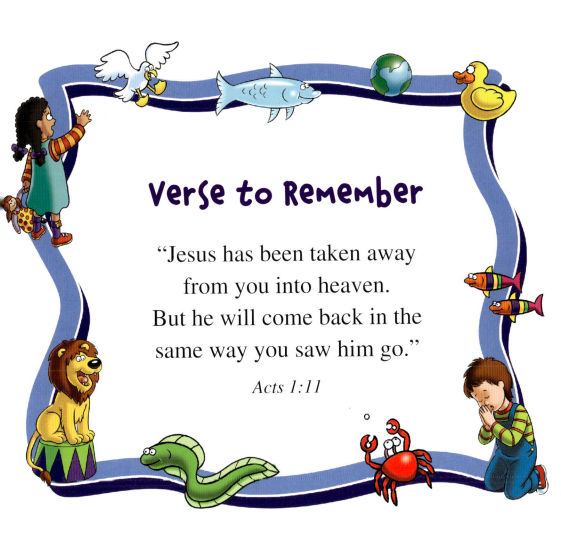

Verse to Remember

"Jesus has been taken away
from you into heaven.
But he will come back in the
same way you saw him go."

Acts 1:11

How to Go to Heaven

Look at the little boy in the picture. He is doing something nice for his grandma. He is getting her some soup for her lunch.

Some people think that doing good things is what allows them to go to heaven. But the Bible says that believing in Jesus is the only way to go to heaven.

God loved the world so much that he gave his one and only Son. Anyone who believes in him will not die but will have eternal life.

John 3:16

Jesus answered, "I am the way and the truth and the life. No one comes to the Father except through me."

John 14:6

The most important part about being a Christian is believing that Jesus died to save us from our sins and then rose from the dead. God is happy when we do good things for other people.

But God wants us to love him above all, and believe that Jesus died to save us from our sins. When we trust in Jesus and believe that he loves us and ask him to forgive our sins, we know that our sins will be forgiven. Then, when our life on earth is over, we will go to heaven.

Prayer

Dear God,
It's not the good things that I do that
will allow me to go to heaven some day.
I'll go to heaven because I believe in you,
and because I know that Jesus died and
rose again to save me from my sins.
God, please help me to do what's right
every day, just because I know how
much it pleases you. I thank you that
some day I will see you in heaven.
Amen.

Verse to Remember

Anyone who believes
in Jesus will not die but
will have eternal life.

John 3:16

The bestselling Bible Storybook of our time – over 5 million Sold!

Hardcover • 196mm x 164mm, 512pp
ISBN 978 1 85985 554 6
Available at your
local bookstore!

For even more Bible fun, open up the bestselling classic – *The Beginner's Bible*®. With vibrant art and compelling text, more than 90 Bible stories come to life. Kids ages 6 and under will enjoy the fun illustrations of Noah helping the elephant onto the ark, Jonah praying inside the fish, and more as they discover *The Beginner's Bible*® just like millions of children before.

Other products available from *The Beginner's Bible*® line:
The Beginner's Bible® *Gift Edition*   978 1 85985 607 9
The Beginner's Bible® *Noah's Busy Ark*   978 1 85985 600 0

CANDLE
BOOKS